Peter Levi is a poet and a student o
books, including a History of Greek
and a life of Shakespeare. He has t
Gospel.

He was a Fellow of St Catherine's College, Oxfo
spent most of his life, and in the eighties was Professor of Poetry at
Oxford for five years. His lectures about poets, about mystical and
anonymous poets, and about the art itself were published as *The Art of
Poetry* (1991). He has always been fond of *The Revelation of John*
and nourished a despairing wish to make a convincing modern
translation of it.

He lives in Gloucestershire in a cottage looking up a very long village
green near the Gloucester and Sharpness Canal, from which vantage
point he is writing an enormous life of Tennyson.

Other translations and works of philosophy available from Kyle Cathie include:

*The Jewish Mystics* – Rabbi Louis Jacobs
*Tao Te Ching* – Stephen Mitchell
*The Book of Job* – Stephen Mitchell
*George Fox and the Children of Light* – Jonathan Fryer
*The Neoplatonists* – John Gregory
*The English Mystics* – Karen Armstrong

# THE
# REVELATION
# OF JOHN

Translated and
introduced by
PETER LEVI

KYLE CATHIE LIMITED

*For my sister Gillian*

First published in Great Britain in 1992 by
Kyle Cathie Limited
3 Vincent Square London SW1P 2LX

ISBN 1 85626 052 6

A CIP catalogue record for this book is available
from the British Library.

Designed by Beverley Waldron
Typeset by DP Photosetting, Aylesbury, Bucks
Printed and bound by Biddles Ltd, Guildford

# INTRODUCTION

THE FIRST THING to be said about the Book of the Revelation of John is that books of this apocalyptic kind were a Jewish speciality that proliferated about the time of Christ. Those who wish to track down the origins of this entire kind of writings must become familiar not only with the Prophets, but with the Qumran scrolls, and the so-called Sibylline Oracles, which are mostly prophetic works in atrocious Greek verse. The Roman poet Horace quotes one, as if it were familiar to his readers, about Rome falling by its own force (the Greek word *Rome* means force or strength). It is interesting that this pun works only in Greek, setting up the surmise that such literature was essentially a Greek-speaking, anti-Roman product.

But a lifetime of study will not quite explain away the amazing invasion of the New Testament by this full-blooded Jewish document, with its almost pre-Christian Messiah, in its beautiful Greek dress. When Europe innocently sought a classical origin for everything, in the seventeenth century, scholars took a different line. H.J. Grierson in an introduction to *Paradise Lost* (Florence Press, 1925) quotes an early pamphlet by Milton (1641) as follows: "And the Apocalypse of St John is the majestic Image of a high and stately Tragedy, shutting up and intermingling her solemn Scenes and Acts with a seven-fold Chorus of Hallelujas and harping Symphonies: and this my opinion the grave authority of Pareus, commenting that book, is sufficient to confirm."

No doubt Revelation has some effect on the Miltonic God, but this analysis does not really work. Revelations are ragbags, they are not well organised. One of the Qumran scrolls introduces Roman infantry tactics into Armageddon, and certain features of the New Jerusalem in the present work, the four-square layout and the central food and water, reflect Hellenistic and even fifth century BC Greek town planning.

I have thought about translating the Apocalypse, as I was brought up to call it, for years, but the difficulties have always seemed mountainous. What is attractive about it is the most formidable difficulty: it is written in language that is both stylised and vernacular, apparently by someone illiterate at least in Greek, but more likely (to judge from his extremely odd syntax) in all languages. It is like the product of a passionate peasant revivalist from some cultural backwater like medieval Crete. I admire it wholeheartedly. I even believe it, because it takes you by the throat in the manner we are more used to in the poems of Blake.

But there is no sense in pretending that this book is just a poem. In fact it is not a poem at all, though it often comes close to the techniques of poetry, as much of the Bible does. It is written in a prose we no longer possess in English, more heightened in some ways than our poetry ever is. But even if it were written in language we could deal with more easily, and towards which after all any honestly modern translation must tend to reduce it, the whole point of the book as literature is that it claims an authority that lies beyond literature. This is not the peculiar tone or personal style of

God, but rather as if God in choosing to inspire human language had inspired a parody of Himself. This book is indeed inspired, at least in that it is perfectly genuine.

It is also very queer indeed. It is repetitive in places, making nonsense of what it has just said. It is not a single clear allegory, and the scheme which a patient reader may seek with pencil and paper to follow out will lead him only to chase his own tail. The number seven, for example, seems to offer the key. I recollect the elderly Jesuit mystic Father Martindale in his lectures to novices building the most splendid and convincing construction on the number seven: the seven-branched candlestick, the seven churches of Asia and then the seven trumpets, which I think become muddled towards the end. But in a later lecture he had to explain that the original clarity had got confused. I do not know if he liked the idea of an interpolator or an over-active copyist. Some quite simple faults would be explained by the introduction of a copyist: words that seem to be missing or to be added unnecessarily, one or two sentences without main verbs, which in translation one attempts to patch, and so on.

The most astonishing thing about Revelation is its intense moral clarity. It is written from the point of view of Christians persecuted by the Roman empire, mostly about those who have been tortured and executed, and it is addressed to those who will follow them through the same horrible sufferings. Its camaraderie has a touch of the resistance movement, and a complete confidence in Heaven.

Its origins are Jewish, like those of the rest of the New Testament, but I see no precise evidence that it was written by a Jewish Christian. In fact, I would myself guess that he was an Asian, conscious of nomads and of deserts and of the Euphrates, who took a stern view of the cities of the coast. He wrote, I take it, after the fall of Jerusalem, and those scholars may be right who say that using the old numerical system of letters that was normal before signs for numbers were invented, A' = 1, B' = 2, etc., the number 666 means Nero. That would date the Revelation in the middle of the first century AD, and explain why some of it is not so much in the traditional style of prophecy but in code. Nero would not have taken it lying down.

In fact, chapter eighteen in particular is the most thrilling condemnation of Rome, or of any great ancient city, that has come down to us. It is not possible to understand Rome or its equivalent just by reading Livy and Virgil: you must remember chapter eighteen of the Revelation of John. The city is called Babylon, but that is only because we all know the story of Belshazzar's feast, and how Babylon ended. Babylon means Rome. What makes the condemnation so powerful is that it is phrased as a lament: John or the angel he has invented really loves the civilised city. The thud of his disapproval comes at the end of a long, bizarre, wonderful list of luxuries, and unfortunately there is a difficulty about translating it.

It should end "bodies, and the souls of men", and "bodies" has been taken to mean slaves. That is how Jerome's Latin renders it, with the word *mancipiorum*. If that is right, it is important, because it would be the clearest direct condemnation of slavery in the whole New Testament. On the other hand, "bodies and souls of men" is a tempting translation, and as the climax of a list of the luxuries of Babylon it is not without force. But "body and soul" is not so common a phrase in the Bible as it is to us, and personally I am reluctant to abandon "slaves and the souls of men".

I give this as just one example of the impossible difficulties of translating this strong, strange, beautiful text. Another is the twelve stones of the New Jerusalem. I have always wondered what they were, since I was thrilled by them as a boy at boarding school in the 1940s. They are a very odd list, and I imagine their meaning is in some cabbalism of colour or of number, perhaps in a language into which I cannot translate them. I have left their traditional names, semi-intelligible and semi-precious, in the hope that someone as ignorant and as spellbound as I was may find them fascinating as I once did.

It is a curious exercise to see which parts of the vision have passed into folk-memory and which have not. No one now remembers the intricate multiplications by seven or twelve, and no one cares any more what a "cubit" or a "span" is, though "span" does seem to exist in English as a "hand", the measurement of a horse. But from the whole book we remember the word "Alleluia", which is the Hebrew for "Praise God", and bits of Handel that go with it. We know Armageddon, and the four horsemen of the Apocalypse, and perhaps the trees and the water springs of the magic city, which I am tempted to call Oz. I have never forgotten that there will be no more sea, though I had quite forgotten that night would also be abolished. The glassy or glass-like sea which is the floor of Heaven has caused me consternation since childhood. Everyone remembers Patmos, that frugal and skeletal island, and the seven churches of Asia. That must be nearly all. The angel trumpeters and the seven strokes or "plagues" and the creatures with seven horns and ten heads are less memorable, though most people remember something about the book of life, and the unsealing of a book and the Lamb upon his throne.

What is usually utterly forgotten, and therefore quite fresh, is the momentum, the sheer drive and the accumulative power of the book. Who knows or cares how many visions it is or was? They strike so swiftly on each other's heels, and the images are so intimately and invisibly related, that they are like the waves of the sea. Rhetoric is too thin a word for them, because there is something fussy and minutely manipulative about rhetoric. These visions are not like great poetry either, because they are not exploited and the poet virtually never intrudes. They are more like the purest raw material of a great poet. It is noticeable that nothing much is explained. We are told simply of "a man's measure, that is an angel's" (or is that a scholarly interpolation?) and there are a few knowing nudges about politics, but that is all. The altar and the throne and the four living creatures are flatly given, like historical data.

Angels merit more study than they usually get. They can blow trumpets, wage war and ride horses, and one might be tempted to worship one, but his reaction to worship is laconic and horrified. *Hora me* means Stop it, don't do that. Watch out. See you don't do that. There are a number of questions one might ask about the New Jerusalem too, but it is not sensible to ask them. One is not meant to pause in a pedantic way; the best one can do is read it all again, and let it sink in, as the light of the amazing city mysteriously illuminates distant and unnamed nations.

There is no simple scheme to which the vision can logically be reduced, so that one would expect it to have been neglected by the medieval commentaries. But those centuries immediately and intuitively accepted the language of images. To my own considerable surprise, the horse-lion, with its numerous heads and horns, makes an elegant and rather beautiful illustration: I best remember the thirteenth-century Douce Apocalypse at Oxford. And as one might have expected, twelfth-century bestiaries offer creatures almost indistinguishable from those in the Revelation of John. I do not think I am in most ways more credulous than other people, but I feel at home with these beasts and cheered up by them, where the text terrifies me. Whoever wrote it knew all about the threat that the Romans so rightly feared, of a gap in the frontier that would "let in the nomads". But the strangest transformation of all these manuscripts is one of the most moving. In a series of late medieval manuscripts, confined so far as I know (which is not far) to English scribal centres, the hero of the Revelation is a Christ conceived as a contemporary human being, a Piers Plowman, almost exactly St Francis with the marks of Christ on his hands and feet.

It may be that whoever devised these drawings was thinking of the famous *stigmata* that were inflicted on St Francis by an angel, and of the various strange references to the mark of the Lamb or the Beast on one's forehead or forearm. Their real explanation, which no one would have known in the late Middle Ages, is quite simple. There was a real custom in late antiquity, in an age of great cities, when one's religion might be secret or better kept secret, to carry the mark of one's private god tattooed on one's body. The devout would also wear a ring for their god, or occasionally a shackle. It is perfectly possible that some secret symbol, such as the Christian fish which I have seen on a ring from Egypt, would have to be shown before a stranger could be admitted to Communion.

Unfashionable as its tendencies may be in other ways, there is no doubt that the Book of Revelation is intended to be the possession of a community, to instruct and warn and guide its members towards what will happen when the great modern city called Babylon has fallen. I do not think it mattered much what was said about the final state of man, which was described in symbolic terms that are as moving as they are hard to interpret. The point was to get there, and it is clear enough that the seven strokes the angels shook out of their bottles were vague as well as terrible: what the book taught was that survival was by loyalty and faith. John does not go into that in detail either, because he is writing for martyrs. The word martyr, by the way, which I have normally translated as witness, has a range of meanings, and evidently it already had them when John wrote. It is one of those accepted "ecclesiastical terms" which translators of the Bible have been forced to accept. Communion, Baptism and Church are others. Any desacralising word for them loses more than it gains. Witness is a more difficult case, because it often gains by its legal overtones, yet there is no doubt that the Book of Revelation was intended to introduce Christians to their martyrdom. It offered them a framework within which martyrdom on a terrible scale would be acceptable. It still rings like a trumpet-blast. I am as amazed by it today as ever I was. Matthew Arnold's Rugby Chapel and Mr Attlee's socialist England do not distract one's eyes for long from the fall of Babylon.

PETER LEVI
21 June 1991

NOTE

Finally, the only verbal worry that continues to nag me is the Greek word *Ouai*, pronounced *Oo-why*, meaning woe, or alas. Those two words are rather out of use and suggest Frankie Howerd, and anyway alas does not fit phrases like "the third *Ouai*". But it is also a bird's cry, uttered in this book by eagles or vultures. Of course it is meant to be onomatopoeic, like the cawing of a crow. So I have adopted "cry" as the nearest bird-crying equivalent. *Ouai* has no real meaning, it is just a cry.

# THE
# REVELATION
# OF
# JOHN

# CHAPTER
# 1

THE REVELATION OF Jesus Christ which God gave him to reveal to his slaves, which must happen swiftly; and he gave orders, sending through his angel to his slave John, who witnessed to the word of God and to the witnessing of Jesus Christ, as much as he knew. Happy the reader and the hearers of the words of this prophecy and those who keep the things written in it; because the time is near.

John to the seven churches in Asia: grace to you and peace from him that is and was and is to come; and from the seven spirits which are in front of his throne; and from Jesus Christ, the faithful witness, the first-born of the dead and lord of the kings of the earth. To him that loves us and set us free from our sins in his blood, and made us a kingdom, priests of God who is his father: to him be glory and power for ages of ages, amen. Look, he is coming among the clouds, and every eye will see him, and those who pierced him will see him, and all the tribes of the earth will grieve for him. Yes, amen.

I am the A and the Z, says the Lord God, who is and was and is to come, the all mighty.

I, John, your brother and sharer in suffering and kingship

and patience in Jesus, was in the island called Patmos because of the word of God and the witnessing of Jesus. I was in the spirit on the Lord's day, and heard behind me a great voice like a trumpet, saying, Write what you see in a book, and send it to the seven churches: to Ephesos and to Smyrna, and to Pergamon, and to Thyateira, and to Sardis, and to Philadelpheia, and to Laodicea.

And I turned round to see what voice was talking to me. And as I turned I saw seven golden lights, and in the middle of the lights someone like a son of man, dressed full length, and tied with a golden girdle at the breasts. And his head and hair were as white as white wool, like snow, and his eyes were like a flame of fire, and his feet like fine brass, like something molten in a furnace, and his voice like the voice of many waters. And in his right hand he held seven stars, and out of his mouth came a broad sword, double-edged and sharp, and his glance was like the sun when the sun appears in his power. And when I saw him I fell down at his feet like a dead man, and he laid his right hand on me, saying, Do not be afraid. I am the first and the last, and I live, and I became dead, and see, I live and shall live for ages of ages, and I have the keys of death and of the underworld. Therefore write down what you have seen, the things that are now, and the things that will happen after these: the mystery of the seven stars that you saw at my right hand, and the seven golden lights. The seven stars are angels of the seven churches, and the seven lights are the seven churches.

# CHAPTER
## 2

WRITE TO THE angel of the church in Ephesos:

These are the words of the holder of the seven stars in his right hand, who walks in the middle of the seven golden lights. I know your actions and your weariness and patience, and that you cannot bear the wicked, and you tested those who call themselves apostles and are not, and found them out as liars, and you have patience and have borne a burden for my name, and have not been wearied. But I hold it against you that you have lost your first love. Therefore remember what you have fallen from, and be converted, and do as you did at first; if not I am coming to you, and I shall remove your light from its place, if you are not converted. But you have this to be said for you, that you hate the actions of the Nikolaïtes, which I hate too. Whoever has ears, let him hear what the Spirit says to the churches. Whoever wins, I will give him food from the wood of the tree of life, which is in the paradise of God.

And write to the angel of the church in Smyrna:

These are the words of the first and the last, who was dead and lived. I know your anguish and poverty (but you are rich) and the blasphemy of those who say they are Jews and are not, but they are the synagogue of Satan. Do not be afraid of what you are going to suffer. Look, the devil is going to throw some of you into prison, so that you are tested, and you shall have ten days of anguish. Be faithful to the death, and I will give you the crown of life. Whoever has ears, let him hear what the Spirit says to the churches. Whoever wins will suffer no wrong from the second death.

And write to the angel of the church in Pergamon:

These are the words of the holder of the broadsword, double-edged and sharp. I know where you live, where the throne of Satan is, and you keep my name, and you did not deny my faith, even in the days when Antipas my witness and my believer was murdered among you, in the city of Satan. But I have a few things against you, that you have some people there who keep the teaching of Balaam, who taught Balaak to bring scandal to the sons of Israel, the eating of idolatrous sacrifices and fornication: and you have some who keep the teaching of the Nikolaïtes, in just the same way. Therefore be converted, or if not, I am coming to you quickly, and I shall fight with them with the broadsword of my mouth. Whoever has ears, let him hear what the Spirit says to the churches. Whoever wins I will give him some of the hidden manna, and I will give him a white counting-stone, and a new name written on the counting-stone, which no one knows but the one who gets it.

And write to the angel of the church in Thyateira:

These are the words of the Son of God, who has eyes like a flame of fire, and his feet are like fine brass. I know your actions, and your love and faith and service and patience, and your latest actions more than the first. But I have it against you, that you let loose the woman Jezebel, who calls herself a prophetess, and teaches and misleads my people to fornicate and to eat idolatrous sacrifices. And I have given her time to be converted, and she will not be converted from her fornication. Look, I am throwing her into a bed, and those that couple with her into great anguish, if they will not be converted from their actions. And I shall kill her children with death, and all the churches will know that I am the searcher of the testicles and of the heart, and I shall reward each of you according to your actions. But I say to the rest of you at Thyateira, who do not keep that teaching, who have not known the depths of Satan as they say, I am not putting any further weight on you: just keep to what you hold until I come. And whoever wins and keeps to my actions until the end, I shall give him authority over the nations, and he will shepherd them like sheep with a rod of steel, [smashed like earthenware vessels]* just as I got it from my father, and I shall give him the morning star. Whoever has ears, let him hear what the spirit says to the churches.

* As it stands, this phrase makes nonsense of the sentence. It seems to be a reminiscence of the Old Testament. I would delete it. The morning star, the rod and the shepherd seem to go together.

# CHAPTER
## 3

AND WRITE TO the angel of the church in Sardis:

These are the words of the holder of the seven Spirits of God and the seven stars. I know your actions, I know you have the name of being alive, but you are dead. Wake up, and strengthen all that was doing to die, because I have not found your actions perfect in the sight of my God. Therefore remember what you got and what you heard, and keep it and be converted. Because if you do not wake up, I shall come like a burglar, and you will not know what time I am coming to you. But you have a few names in Sardis that have not dirtied their coats, and they shall walk with me dressed in white, because they are worthy to do so. Whoever wins will be dressed like them in white clothing, and I shall not wipe out his name from the book of life, and I shall acknowledge his name in the sight of my father and in the sight of his angels. Whoever has ears, let him hear what the Spirit says to the churches.

And write to the angel of the church in Philadelpheia:

These are the words of the holy, the true, the holder of the key of David, who opens and no man shall close, and who closes and no man opens. I know your actions (look, I have given you a door opened in front of you, which no man is able to shut), for you have little power, and yet you kept to my word and you did not deny my name. Look, I am giving you from the synagogue of Satan those who call themselves Jews, but they are liars and are not Jews; look, I shall make them come to you and bow to the ground in worship at your feet, and understand that I loved you. Because you kept to the word of my patience, and I shall keep you from the time of trial which is about to come for the entire world, to test all those who live on earth. I am coming quickly; hold on to what you have, so that no one can take away your crown. Whoever wins, I shall make him a pillar in the temple of God, and he will not go out any more, and I shall write on him the name of my God, and the name of the city of my God, the New Jerusalem, which comes down out of Heaven from my God, and my name which is New. Whoever has ears let him hear what the Spirit says to the churches.

And write to the angel of the church in Laodicea:

These are the words of Amen, the faithful and true witness, the beginning of God's creation. I know your actions, I know you are neither cold nor hot, it would be better if you were either cold or hot. As it is because you are tepid, and neither hot nor cold, I am going to vomit you out of my mouth. Because you say I am a rich man, I have got rich, and I have no kind of need, and you do not know that you are destitute and pitiable, and poor and blind and naked, I advise you to buy from me gold refined in the fire, to be rich, and white clothing to put on, so that the disgrace of your nakedness is not apparent, and ointment to rub on your eyes, so that you see. I test and train everyone I love, therefore catch fire and be converted. Look, I am standing at the door and knocking; if anyone hears my voice and opens the door, I will come in to him and have dinner with him, and he will have dinner with me. Whoever wins, I will let him sit with me on my throne, just as I won, and I sat down with my father on his throne. Whoever has ears, let him hear what the Spirit says to the churches.

# CHAPTER
# 4

AFTER THAT I looked, and there! a door that was opened in Heaven, and the voice, that I heard at first like a trumpet talking to me, was saying, Come up here, and I will show you what must happen after this. Immediately I was in the spirit, and look, a throne stood in Heaven, and someone sitting on the throne, and the one who sat there seemed to be made of jasper and red cornelian, and around the throne was a rainbow that seemed to be made of emerald, and in a circle round the throne were twenty-four thrones, and on these thrones twenty-four old men were sitting, dressed in white clothing, and with golden crowns on their heads. And out of the throne there came lightnings and voices and thunderings. And there were seven lamps of fire burning before the throne, which are the seven spirits of God, and before the throne as it were a sea of glass, like rock crystal, and in the middle of the throne and all around the throne, four creatures full of eyes in front and behind. And the first creature was like a lion and the second creature was like a young bull, and the third creature had a face like a man's, and the fourth creature was like an eagle in flight. And the four creatures had each one of them six wings upwards and in a circle, and within the circle they were full of eyes, and day and night they never rest from saying Holy, holy, holy, Lord God Almighty, who was and who is and who is to come. And when the creatures give glory and honour and thanksgiving to the one who sits on the throne, who lives for ages and ages, the twenty-four old men will fall down before the one who sits on the throne, and will worship him who lives for ages of ages, and they will throw down their crowns before the throne, saying, Worthy are you, our Lord and our God, to receive glory and honour and power, because you created all things, and through you they were and they were created.

# CHAPTER
# 5

AND I SAW on the right of the one sitting on the throne a book with writing inside and outside, sealed with seven seals, and saw a strong angel proclaiming in a loud voice, Who is worthy to open the book, and to unseal its seven seals? And no one in Heaven or on earth or under the earth could open the book or look at it. And I wept very much, because no one was found worthy to open the book, or to look at it; and one of the old men said to me, Do not weep: look, the lion from the tribe of Juda, the stem of David, has won, he will open the book and the seven seals on it. And I saw in the middle of the throne and the four creatures, and in the middle of the old men, a lamb standing there slaughtered, with seven horns and seven eyes, which are the seven spirits of God, sent out over all the earth. And he came and took the book from the one who was sitting on the throne. And when he took it, the four creatures and the twenty-four old men fell down in front of the lamb, they all had a stringed instrument and gold pots full of incense, which are the prayers of the saints. And they sang a new song, saying You are worthy to take the book, and open its seals, because you were slaughtered, and you bought for

God with your blood those of every tribe and language and people and nation, and made them a kingdom and a priesthood for our God, and they shall be kings over the earth. And I looked, and heard the voice of many angels encircling the throne and the creatures and the old men, and their number was hundreds of millions and thousands of thousands, saying in loud voices, Worthy is the Lamb who was slaughtered to get power and riches and wisdom and strength and honour and glory and blessing. And I heard every creature which is in Heaven and on earth and under the earth and on the sea, and everything that is in them, saying, Blessing and honour, glory and power to him that sits on the throne, and to the Lamb, for ages of ages. And the four creatures said, Amen, and the old men fell down and worshipped.

# CHAPTER
# 6

AND I SAW when the Lamb opened one of the seven seals, and I heard one of the four creatures saying in a voice like thunder, Come, and I watched, and look, a white horse, and the rider had a bow, and he was given a crown, and he went out as a winner and he went to win.

And when he opened the second seal, I heard the second creature say, Come. And another horse came out, a chestnut, and the rider was commissioned to take away peace from the earth so that they would slaughter one another; and he was given a great sword.

And when he opened the third seal, I heard the third creature saying, Come. And I watched, and look, a black horse, and its rider had a balance in his hand. And I heard a voice in the middle of the four creatures saying, A cup of wheat for a penny, and three cups of barley for a penny, and do no damage to the oil or the wine.

And when he opened the fourth seal, I heard the voice of the fourth creature, saying, Come. And I watched, and look, a green horse, and the name of his rider was death, and hell went with him, and he was given authority over a quarter of the earth to kill with the sword and with famine and with death and by the beasts of the earth.

And when he opened the fifth seal, I saw below the altar the souls of those who were murdered for the word of God and for the witness that they gave, and they cried out in a loud voice, saying, How long, Lord, holy and true, until you judge and avenge our blood on the inhabitants of the earth? And each of them was given white clothing and they were told to rest a little while longer, until the number of their fellow-slaves and their brothers, who would be killed as they had been, should be complete.

And I watched when he opened the sixth seal, and there was a great earthquake, and the sun turned as black as a horsehair cloth, and the moon all bloody, and the stars of Heaven fell down on to the earth, like a fig tree dropping unripe figs when a great wind shakes it. And Heaven was gone like a scroll rolled up, and every mountain and island was moved from its place. And the kings of the earth, and the moguls and the commanders and the rich and the strong, and every slave and every free man hid themselves in caves and rock crannies in the mountains, and they said to the mountains and the rocks, Fall on us, and hide us from the face of him that sits on the throne, and from the anger of the Lamb, because the great day of their anger has come, and who can stand?

# CHAPTER
# 7

AFTER THAT I saw four angels standing at the four corners of the earth, controlling the four winds of the earth, so that no wind should blow on earth, neither over the sea nor at any tree. And I saw another angel going up out of the rising sun, holding the seal of the living God; and he cried out in a loud voice to the four angels who were given power to harm the earth and the sea, saying, Do no harm to the earth or the sea or the trees, while we seal the slaves of our God on their foreheads. And I heard the number of those who were sealed: a hundred and forty-four thousand were sealed from every tribe of the sons of Israel.

From the tribe of Juda there were twelve thousand sealed, from the tribe of Ruben twelve thousand, from the tribe of Gad twelve thousand, from the tribe of Aser twelve thousand, from the tribe of Nephthalim twelve thousand, from the tribe of Manasses twelve thousand, from the tribe of Symeon twelve thousand, from the tribe of Levi twelve thousand, from the tribe of Issachar twelve thousand, from the tribe of Zaboulon twelve thousand, from the tribe of Joseph twelve thousand, from the tribe of Benjamin twelve thousand sealed. After that I watched, and look, a great crowd which no man could number, from every nation and tribe and people and language, standing in front of the throne and in front of the Lamb, wearing white clothing and with palms in their hands; and they cried out in a loud voice, saying, Salvation to our God who sits on the throne, and to the Lamb. And all the angels stood round the throne and round the old men and the four creatures, and they fell on their faces before the throne, and worshipped God, saying, Amen, blessing and glory and wisdom and thanksgiving and honour and power and strength to our God for ages of ages. Amen. And one of the old men answered and said to me, Who are these who are dressed in white clothing? And I said to him, Sir, you know. And he said to me, They are those who have come from great suffering, and washed their clothes, and whitened them in the blood of the Lamb. Because of this they face the throne of God, and worship him day and night in his temple, and he that sits on the throne will pitch his tent among them. They will not be hungry any more, or thirsty any more, nor will the sun fall on them nor any burning heat, because the Lamb in the middle of the throne will be their shepherd, and he will take them to the springs of the water of life, and God will wipe away every tear from their eyes.

# CHAPTER
# 8

AND WHEN HE opened the seventh seal, there was silence in Heaven for half an hour. And I saw the seven angels who stand before God, and they were given seven trumpets.

And another angel came and stood at the altar, with a golden pot for incense, and he was given a lot of incense to offer with the prayers of all the saints at the golden altar facing the throne. And the smoke of the incense went up with the prayers of the saints from the hand of the angel who faces God. And the angel took the incense pot and filled it from the altar fire and threw it on the earth. And there were thunderings and voices and lightnings and earthquake.

And the seven angels with the seven trumpets got ready to sound their trumpets.

And the first trumpet sounded, and there came hail and fire mingled with blood, and they were flung down on to the earth, and a third of the earth was burnt up, and a third of the trees were burnt up, and all the green grass was burnt up.

And the second angel's trumpet sounded, and a great mountain flaming with fire was flung into the sea, and a third of the sea turned to blood, and a third of the creatures that are in the sea died, those that have souls, and a third of the ships were destroyed.

And the third angel's trumpet sounded, and a great star burning like a light fell out of Heaven, and it fell on a third of the rivers and the springs of water, and the name of that star is Wormwood, and a third of the water turned as bitter as wormwood, and many men died of the water, because they were pickled by it.

And the fourth angel's trumpet sounded, and a third of the sun and a third of the moon and a third of the stars were struck, so that a third of them were darkened, and for a third of her time day did not appear, and night increased likewise.

And I looked, and I heard an eagle flying in midheaven, saying in a loud voice, Cry, cry, cry for the inhabitants of the earth, because of the rest of the trumpet voices of the three angels who are ready to sound.

# CHAPTER
# 9

AND THE FIFTH angel's trumpet sounded, and I saw a star that had fallen out of Heaven on to the earth, and he was given the key to the well-shaft of the abyss, and he opened the well-shaft of the abyss, and smoke came up from the well-shaft like the smoke of a great furnace, and the sun and the air were darkened from the smoke of the well-shaft. And locusts came out of the smoke on to the earth, and they were given authority as the scorpions of the earth have authority. And they were told not to harm the grass of the earth or any greenery or any tree, but only men who do not have the seal of God on their foreheads. And they were allowed not to kill them, but to torture them for five months; and their torture was like a scorpion's torture when it stings a man. And in those days men shall seek for death and they shall not find him, and they shall desire to die and death shall escape from them. And the kind of thing the locusts shall be is like horses ready for battle, with crowns of gold on their heads, and with faces like the faces of men. And they had hair like women's hair, and their teeth were like lions' teeth. And they had breast-plates like iron breast-plates, and the noise of their wings was like the noise of chariots and many horses galloping to war. And they had tails like scorpions, and stings, and in their tails is their authority to harm mankind for five months. They have a king over them, the angel of the abyss; his name in Hebrew is Abaddon, and in Greek his name is Apollyon, the Destroyer.

That was the end of the first cry, but look, here come two more cries after that.

And the sixth angel sounded his trumpet, and I heard a voice from the horns of the altar of gold that faces God, saying to the sixth angel, Let loose the four angels who are tied down on the great river, Euphrates. And the four angels were let loose, prepared for the hour and the day and the month and the year, to kill one third of mankind. And the number of cavalry soldiers was two hundred million: I heard their number. And so in my vision I saw the horses and the riders with breast-plates of fire and hyacinth and sulphur, and the heads of the horses like lion-heads, and fire and smoke and sulphur came out of their mouths. From these three blows one third of mankind died, from the fire and smoke and sulphur that came out of their mouths. Because the power of the horses is in their mouths and in their tails, because their tails are like snakes, which have heads and do the harm. And the remnant of mankind, who were not killed by these blows, were not sorry for their actions: they did not stop worshipping devils, and idols of gold and silver and bronze and stone and wood, which are unable to see or hear or walk about; and they were not sorry for their murders or their drugs or their fornication or their thievery.

# CHAPTER
# 10

AND I SAW another strong angel coming down out of Heaven, dressed in cloud, with the rainbow on his head and his face like the sun, and his feet like pillars of fire, and in his hand he held an open book; and he put down his right foot on the sea and his left on the land, and cried out in a loud voice just as a lion roars; and when he cried out, the seven thunders spoke in their own voices. And when the seven thunders spoke, I was going to write, and I heard a voice from Heaven saying, Seal up what the seven thunders spoke, and do not write it down. And the angel I saw standing on the sea and on the land raised his right hand to Heaven, and swore by him who lives for ages of ages, who created Heaven and what is in it, and earth and what is in it, and the sea and what is in it, that time will no longer exist, but in the days of the voice of the seventh angel, when he is about to sound his trumpet the mystery of God shall be completed, as he said in his gospel to the prophets who are his slaves. And the voice I heard from Heaven spoke again behind me, saying, Come, take the book which is open in the hand of the angel standing on the sea and on the earth. And I went to the angel and told him to give me the book.

And he said to me, Take it and eat it up, and it will be bitter in your belly, but in your mouth it will be as sweet as honey, and I took the book from the angel's hand, and ate it up, and it was as sweet as honey in my mouth, and when I ate it my belly was bitter. And they said to me, You must prophesy again over many peoples and nations and languages and kings.

# CHAPTER
# 11

AND I WAS given a reed like a stick, with the words, Get up and measure the temple of God, and the altar, and the worshippers in it. And leave out the court outside the temple, and do not measure it, because it has been given to the nations, and they shall walk in the holy city for forty-two months. And I will let my two witnesses prophesy for one thousand two hundred and sixty days, dressed in coarse cloth. These are the two olive trees and the two lamps which stand in front of the Lord of the earth. And if anyone seeks to harm them, fire shall come out of their mouths and consume their enemies; and if anyone seeks to harm them, that is how he must die. They have the power to close Heaven so that rain does not fall in the days of their prophecy. And they have power over the waters, to turn them to blood, and to strike the earth with every blow as often as they wish. And when they complete their witnessing, the beast that comes up from the abyss will go to war with them, and conquer them, and kill them. And their dead bodies shall lie in the square of the great city which is called in spirit Sodom and Egypt, where their master was crucified. And men of the peoples and tribes and languages and nations shall see their dead bodies for three and a half days, and they will not let their bodies be put into a tomb. And the inhabitants of the earth will be glad about them and celebrate, and send one another presents, because these two prophets tormented the inhabitants of the earth. And after three and a half days the spirit of life entered into them from God, and they stood up on their feet, and a great fear fell on those who observed them. And they heard a loud voice from Heaven saying to them, Come up here. And they went up into Heaven in a cloud, and their enemies watched them. And in that hour there was a great earthquake, and a tenth of the city fell, and seven thousand men by name were killed in the earthquake; and the rest were terrified, and gave glory to the God of Heaven.

That was the end of the second cry, but look, the third cry comes quickly.

And the seventh angel's trumpet sounded, and there were loud voices in Heaven, saying, The kingdom of the world of our Lord and of his Anointed has come, and he shall reign for ages of ages. And the twenty-four old men, who sit on their thrones facing God, fell down on their faces and worshipped God, saying, We thank you, Lord God Almighty, who is and who was, for taking your great power into your hands, and for reigning. And the nations became angry, and your anger has come and the time has come for the dead to be judged, and for your slaves the prophets and the saints and those who fear your name great and small to be given their wages, and for the destruction of the destroyers of the earth.

And the temple of God which is in Heaven was opened, and the ark of his testament was seen in his temple, and there were lightnings and voices and thunderings and earthquake and a great hailstorm.

# CHAPTER
# 12

AND A GREAT sign was seen in Heaven, a woman dressed in the sun, with the moon under her feet and a crown of twelve stars under her feet, and she was pregnant; and she cried out in labour, in torment to give birth. And another sign was seen in Heaven, and look, a great fiery dragon with seven heads and ten horns, and seven crowns on its heads. And his tail swept away a third of the stars of Heaven, and threw them down on to the earth. And the dragon stood facing the woman who was about to give birth, to eat her child when she bore it. And she bore a son who shall rule all nations with a rod of steel, and her child was snatched away to God and to his throne. And the woman escaped into the desert, where she had a place prepared for her by God, where they could look after her for one thousand two hundred and sixty days.

And there was war in Heaven; Michael and his angels fought against the dragon, and the dragon and his angels fought but they did not win, and no place was found for them any more in Heaven. And the great dragon, the ancient serpent, who is called the devil and Satan, who wanders over the whole universe, was hit, and his angels were hit with him. And I heard a loud voice in Heaven that said, Now the salvation and power and kingdom of our God, and the authority of his Anointed, have taken place, because the accuser of our brothers, who accused them day and night in the presence of God, has been struck down. And they have beaten him through the blood of the Lamb, and through the word of their witnessing; they did not love their own soul but suffered their own death. Because of this be glad, you Heavens and all who live in them; cry for the earth and the sea, because the devil has gone down to you in furious anger, knowing that his time is short.

And when the dragon saw that it was struck down to the earth, it went after the woman who had given birth to a son. And the woman was given the two wings of the great eagle, to fly to the desert to her own place, where she was protected for a time and times and half a time, from the face of the snake. And the snake spat out of his mouth behind the woman water like a river to carry her away. And the earth helped the woman, and earth opened her mouth and drank down the river that the dragon spat out of his mouth. And the dragon was angry with the woman, and went away to fight a war with the rest of her offspring, with those who obey the commands of God and keep hold of the witnessing of Jesus. And it stood on the sand beside the sea.

# CHAPTER
# 13

AND I SAW a beast coming up out of the sea, with ten horns and seven heads, and ten crowns on the horns and names on its heads that are a blasphemy. And the beast I saw was like a leopard, and its feet were like a bear's, and its mouth was a lion's mouth; and the dragon gave it his own power, and his throne, and great authority. And one of its heads seemed to be massacred to death, and its death wound was cured, and the whole earth was amazed at the beast, and they worshipped the snake, because it gave authority to the beast, and they worshipped the beast, and said, Who is there like the beast? And who can fight with him? And it was given a mouth uttering great things and blasphemies. And it was given authority to do that for forty-two months. And it opened its mouth to blaspheme against God, to blaspheme his name and his dwelling and all those who live in Heaven. And it was permitted to go to war with the saints, and to conquer them, and it was given authority over every tribe and people and language and nation. And all the inhabitants of the earth will worship him, all whose name is not written in the book of life of the Lamb who was slaughtered from the beginning of the world. Whoever has ears, let him hear. Whoever takes prisoners shall be a prisoner; whoever kills with the knife must die by the knife. This is the patience and the faith of the saints.

And I saw another beast coming up out of the earth, with two horns like a lamb, and it uttered like a snake, and it had all the authority of the first beast in its presence. And it made the earth and its inhabitants worship the first beast, whose death-wound was healed. And it did great miracles, and made fire out of Heaven come down on to the earth in the sight of men. And it seduced the inhabitants of the earth through the miracles it was permitted to do in the sight of the beast, telling the inhabitants of the earth to make an image of the beast who suffered the knife-wound and lived. And it was permitted to give spirit to the image of the beast, so that the image uttered, and to make anyone who did not worship the image of the beast be killed. And it made everyone, great and small, rich and poor, free men and slaves, be given a mark on their right hands or on their foreheads, so that no one could buy or sell unless he had this mark of the name of the beast or the number of his name. This is wisdom. Whoever has a brain, let him calculate the number of the beast, because it is a man's number, and his number is 666.

# CHAPTER
# 14

AND I WATCHED, and look, the Lamb standing on Mount Sion, and a hundred and forty-four thousand men with him, and his name and the name of his father written on their foreheads. And I heard a voice from Heaven like the voice of many waters, and like the voice of a great thunderstorm; and the voice I heard was like the players of stringed instruments playing on their instruments, and they seemed to sing a new song in the sight of the throne, and in the sight of the four creatures and the old men. And no one could learn the song except the hundred and forty-four thousand who were brought from the earth. These are the ones who were not polluted with women, because they are virgins. These follow the Lamb wherever he goes. They were bought from mankind as a first and pure offering to God and to the Lamb. And no lie was found in their speech, they are innocent.

And I saw another angel flying in midheaven, with an everlasting gospel to tell the people on earth, and every nation and tribe and language and people, saying in a loud voice, Fear God, and give him glory, because the hour of his judgement has come, and worship him who made Heaven and earth and sea and the springs of waters.

And another second angel followed him, saying, She has fallen, great Babylon has fallen, who made all nations drunk with the cursed wine of her fornication.

And another third angel followed them, saying in a loud voice, Whoever worships the beast and its image, and takes the mark on his forehead or on his hand, he shall be given a drink of the wine of the anger of God, which has been stirred unmixed in the cup of his furious anger, and he shall be tormented in fire and sulphur in the sight of the holy angels and in the sight of the Lamb, and the smoke of their torment shall rise for ages of ages, and those that worship the beast and his image and whoever takes the mark of his name, shall have no rest day or night. This is the patience of the saints, who obey the commands of God and keep the faith of Jesus.

And I heard a voice from Heaven, saying, Write, Happy are the dead who die in the Lord from now on; yes, says the Spirit, they will rest from their troubles, because their actions will follow them.

And I watched, and look, a white cloud, and someone like a son of man sitting on the cloud, with a golden crown on his head and a sharp sickle in his hand. And another angel came out of the temple, crying out in a loud voice to the one sitting on the cloud, Send in your sickle and reap, because the time for reaping has come, because the harvest of the earth has dried out. And the one who sat on the cloud threw down his sickle on to the earth, and the earth was reaped.

And another angel came out of the temple in Heaven, and he also had a sharp sickle. And another angel came out from the altar with authority over the fire, and shouted in a loud voice to the one with the sharp sickle, saying, Send your sharp sickle and pick the clusters of the vine of the earth, because its grapes are ripe. And the angel threw his sickle on to the earth, and picked the vine of the earth, and threw the grapes into the great wine press of the anger of God. And the press was trodden outside the city, and blood came out of the wine press up to the iron bits of the horses, from one thousand six hundred furlongs.

# CHAPTER
# 15

AND I SAW another great and wonderful sign in Heaven, seven angels with the seven last strokes, because in them the anger of God was complete.

And I saw a sea of glass mingled with fire, and the conquerors of the beast and his image and the number of his name, standing by the glassy sea holding the stringed instruments of God. And they sang the song of Moses the slave of God, and the song of the Lamb, saying, Great and wonderful are your actions, Lord God Almighty, just and true are your ways, King of ages. Who will not fear you, Lord, and glorify your name? Because you alone are holy; because all nations will come and worship in your presence, because your justifications have been made plain.

And after that I looked, and the temple of the dwelling of the witness was opened in Heaven, and the seven angels who held the seven strokes came out of the temple, dressed in pure, bright stone, and belted around the breasts with golden strings. And one of the four creatures gave to the seven angels seven golden bottles full of the anger of God who lives for ages of ages. And the temple was filled with smoke from the glory of God, and from his power; and no

one could enter the temple until the seven strokes of the
seven angels were complete.

# CHAPTER
## 16

AND I HEARD a loud voice from the temple saying to the seven angels, Go and pour out the seven bottles of the anger of God on to the earth.

And the first went and poured out his bottle on to the earth, and an evil and painful ulcer afflicted the men who had the mark of the beast, and the worshippers of his image.

And the second poured out his bottle into the sea, and it turned to blood like dead men's blood, and every soul alive that was in the sea died.

And the third poured out his bottle into the rivers and the springs of the waters, and they turned to blood. And I heard the angel of the waters saying, You are just, you who are and was, the holy one, to have judged these things: because they poured out the blood of saints and of prophets, and you have given them blood to drink; they deserve it. And I heard the altar saying, Yes, Lord God Almighty, your decisions are true and just.

And the fourth poured out his bottle on the sun, and he was allowed to burn mankind with fire. And men were burned in a great conflagration, and they blasphemed the name of God who has authority over these strokes, and they were not converted to give him glory.

And the fifth poured out his bottle on the throne of the beast; and his kingdom was darkened, and they chewed their tongues for anguish, and cursed the God of Heaven for their sufferings and their ulcers, but they were not converted from their actions.

And the sixth one poured out his bottle into the great river, the Euphrates, and its water dried up, for the road of the kings out of the rising sun to be prepared. And I saw three unclean spirits like snakes coming out of the mouth of the dragon, and out of the mouth of the beast, and out of the mouth of the false prophet, because there exist spirits of devils that do miracles, which come out to the kings of the whole world, to gather them together for war on the great day of God almighty. (Look, I am coming like a thief. Happy is the man who is awake and looking after his clothes, so as not to walk about naked and have his ugliness seen.) And he brought them together to the place which in Hebrew is called Harmagedon.

And the seventh one poured out his bottle into the air; and a loud voice came out from the temple, out from the throne, which said, It has happened; and there were lightnings and voices and thunderings, and there was a great earthquake, there has never been one like it since there were men on the earth, not an earthquake like that, not on such a scale. And the great city was split into three parts, and the cities of the nations fell down, and great Babylon came into the mind of God, to give her the cup of the wine of anger of his furious rage. And every island disappeared, and the mountains were not to be found. And a great hailstorm like cannon balls came down out of Heaven on mankind. And men cursed God for the stroke of the hail, because the stroke of it is very great indeed.

# CHAPTER
# 17

AND ONE OF the seven angels with the seven bottles came
and spoke to me, saying, Here, I will show you the
judgement of the great whore who sits on many waters, with
whom the kings of the earth whored, and the inhabitants of
the earth were drunk with the wine of her fornication. And
he carried me away to the desert in the spirit, and I saw a
woman sitting on a crimson beast, full of names that are
blasphemies, with seven heads and ten horns. And the
woman was dressed in purple and crimson and gilded with
gold and precious stone and pearls; she had a golden cup in
her hand full of abominations and the pollutions of her
fornication, and her name is written on her forehead,
Mystery, Babylon the great, mother of the fornications and
abominations of the earth. And I saw the woman drunk
with the blood of the saints, and the blood of the martyrs of
Jesus. And I was stupefied at the sight of her, utterly
stupefied. And the angel said to me, Why are you stupefied?
I will tell you the mystery of the woman, and of the beast
that carries her, that has seven heads and ten horns. The
beast that you saw was and is not, and it is going to climb up
out of the abyss, and go to its destruction. And the

inhabitants of the earth whose name is not written in the book of life from the beginning of the world shall be stupefied when they see the beast, because it was and is not, and yet there it will be. This is the brains of the wise man. The seven heads are seven hills, and the woman sits on them, and there are seven kings, five have fallen, one is now, and the other has not come yet. And when he comes he must stay for a brief while. And the beast which was and is not is both the eighth and one of the seven, and he is going to his destruction. And the ten horns you saw are ten kings who have not reigned yet, but they will take power as kings for an hour, after the beast. They all have the same idea, and they will hand over their power and authority to the beast. They will go to war with the Lamb, and the Lamb will beat them, because he is the lord of lords and king of kings, and his side are chosen and specially chosen and faithful. And he said to me, The waters you saw, where the whore sat, are peoples and mobs and nations and languages. And the ten horns that you saw, and the beast, will hate the whore, and leave her deserted and naked and eat her flesh, and burn her up in a fire. Because God has put it into their hearts to do as he chooses, and agree on the same choice, and hand over their royalty to the beast, until the words of God come true. And the woman that you saw is the great city that has sovereignty over the kings of the earth.

# CHAPTER
# 18

AFTER THIS I saw another angel coming down out of Heaven, with great authority, and the earth was lit up with his glory, and he cried out in a strong voice, and said, She has fallen, great Babylon has fallen, and she has become the estate of devils, and the fortress of every dirty spirit, and the fortress of every dirty and loathsome winged thing. Because all the nations have fallen down from the wine of her whoring, and the kings of the earth whored with her, and the merchants of the earth grew rich on the strength of her delicacies.

And I heard another voice from Heaven saying, Come out of her, my people, do not take part in her sins, and you will not be struck with her strokes; because her sins have mounted up to Heaven, and God has remembered her wickednesses. Give her as she gave, and double what you pay her, act as she acted: mix her double in the same cup that she mixed. She glorified herself and she was delicate, so pay her back the same amount in torment and in grief; because she says in her heart, I am a queen on my throne, and I am not a widow, and I do not know grief. Therefore her punishment shall come in one day, death and grief and famine, and she shall be burnt up with fire, because the Lord God who has judged her is strong. And the kings of the earth who whored with her and were delicate with her shall lament and tear themselves for her, when they see the smoke of her conflagration, standing at a distance for fear of her torments, saying, Cry, cry, Babylon the great city, the strong city, because in one hour your judgement has come. And the merchants of the earth shall cry and grieve over her, because nobody buys their goods any more: goods of gold and silver and precious stone and pearls and fine linen and purple and silk and crimson, and all kinds of eastern wood and all vessels of ivory, and all vessels of most precious wood and bronze and steel and marble, and cinnamon and scent and incense and myrrh and frankincense, and wine and oil and corn, and cattle and sheep, and horses and cars and slaves, and the souls of men. And the fruit that your heart desired has vanished from you, and all that gleamed and glittered has perished from you, and they shall not find those things any more. The merchants of them, and those who grew rich from her, shall stand at a distance for fear of her torments, weeping and grieving, saying, Cry, cry, for the great city, who was dressed in fine linen and purple and crimson, and gilded with gold and precious stones and pearls, because in one hour all that wealth was devastated. And every ship's captain and every merchantman, and sailors, and all those whose work is the sea, stood at a distance, and cried out when they saw the smoke of her fire, and said, What city is like the great city? And they threw dust on their heads and cried out with weeping and with grief, and they said, Cry, cry, the great city, by which everyone who had ships on the sea grew rich from her abundance, has been devastated in one hour. Be glad over her, Heaven, and you saints and apostles and prophets, because God has given judgement against her in your case.

And a strong angel lifted up a stone the size of a millstone, and flung it into the sea, saying, Like that, at one push, Babylon the great city shall be thrown down, and she shall not be found any more. And the sound of stringed instruments and musicians and flute-playing and trumpeters shall no longer be heard in you, and all the craftsmen of every craft shall no longer be found in you, and the sound of the mill shall no longer be heard in you, and the light of a lamp shall no longer shine in you, and the voice of the bridegroom and the bride shall not be heard in you any more; because your merchants were the great of the earth, because with your drugs all the nations were seduced. And in her was found the blood of the prophets and saints and of all who were murdered on the earth.

# CHAPTER
## 19

AFTER THAT I heard the loud voice of a great crowd in Heaven, saying, Alleluia: salvation and glory and power of our God; his judgements are true and just; because he has judged the great whore who corrupted the earth with her whoring, and he has avenged the blood of his slaves that was shed by her. And a second time they said, Alleluia; and her smoke goes up for ages of ages. And the twenty-four old men and the four creatures fell down and worshipped God who sits on the throne, saying, Amen, Alleluia. And a voice came out of the throne saying, Praise our God, all his slaves who fear him, great and small. And I heard something like the voice of a great crowd, and like the voice of numerous waters, and like the voice of powerful thundering, saying Alleluia, because the Lord our God Almighty is king. Let us be glad and happy, and give him the glory; because the wedding of the Lamb has come, and his bride has prepared herself. And she has been allowed to dress in gleaming, pure linen, because the linen is the justice of the saints. And he said to me, Write, blessed are those invited to the dinner of the Lamb. And he said to me, These are the truthful words of God. And I fell down at his feet to worship him, and he said to me, Watch out, do not do that, I am your fellow slave and one of your brothers who keep the witness of Jesus; worship God; because the witness of Jesus is the spirit of prophecy.

And I saw Heaven opened, and look, a white horse, and his rider is called faithful and true, and he judges and goes to war in justice, and his eyes are a flame of fire, and there are many crowns on his head, and he has a name written on him which no one knows but him, and he is dressed in a cloak sprinkled with blood, and his name is the Word of God. And the armies of Heaven followed him on white horses, dressed in pure white linen. And a sharp sword comes out of his mouth to strike the nations, and he herds them with a steel rod, and he treads the wine press of the furious anger of God Almighty. And he has a name written on his cloak and on his thigh, King of Kings and Lord of Lords.

And I saw an angel standing in the sun; and he cried out in a loud voice, speaking to all winged creatures that fly in mid-heaven, Here, gather for the great dinner of God, to eat the flesh of kings, and the flesh of colonels, and the flesh of the strong, and the flesh of horses and their riders, and the flesh of them all, free men and slaves and great and small.

And I saw the beast and the kings of the earth and their armies gathered to go to war with the rider on the horse and with his army. And the beast was caught, and so was the false prophet who did miracles in his presence with which he seduced those who accepted the mark of the beast, and those who worshipped his image. The two of them were thrown living into the lake of fire and burning sulphur, and the rest of them were killed by the sword of the rider on the horse, the sword that comes out of his mouth. And all the flying things gorged themselves on their flesh.

# CHAPTER
## 20

AND I SAW an angel coming down from Heaven, holding the key of the abyss, with a huge chain in his hand. And he took hold of the dragon, the ancient snake who is also the devil and Satan, and tied him for a thousand years, and threw him into the abyss, and turned the key and put a seal on the lock above him, so that he will not seduce the peoples until his thousand years are complete. After that he must be let loose for a short time.

And I saw thrones, and they sat on them, and their judgement was given to them; and all the souls of those who were killed with the axe for the witness of Jesus and the word of God, and who did not worship the beast or his image, and who did not accept his mark on their forehead and on their hand: and they lived, and they reigned as kings with Christ for a thousand years. The rest of the dead did not live until the thousand years were complete. This is the first resurrection. Blessed and holy is he who has a part in the first resurrection. Over them the second death has no power, but they will be priests of God and of Christ, and they shall reign as kings with him for a thousand years.

And when the thousand years are complete, Satan will be

let loose from his prison, and come out to seduce the nations in the four corners of the earth, Gog and Magog, and gather them together for war, and their number will be like the sands of the sea. And they came up on to the surface of the earth, and they encircled the camp of the saints and the beloved city; and fire came down from Heaven and ate them up. And the devil who seduced them was thrown into the same lake of fire and sulphur where the beast and the false prophet were thrown, and they shall be tormented day and night for ages of ages.

And I saw a great shining throne, and him who sat on it, from whose face Heaven and earth fled, and no place was found for them. And I saw the dead great and small, standing in the sight of the throne, and books were opened; and another book was opened, which is the book of life, and the dead were judged by what was written in the books, according to their actions. And the sea gave up the dead that were in her, and death and the underworld gave up the dead that were in them, and everyone was judged according to their actions. And death and the underworld were thrown into the lake of fire: this is the second death, the lake of fire. And whoever was not written in the book of life, they were thrown into the lake of fire.

# CHAPTER
# 21

AND I SAW a new Heaven and a new earth, because the first Heaven and the first earth had vanished, and there was no sea any more. And I saw the holy city, New Jerusalem, coming down out of Heaven from God, prepared like a bride decorated for her husband. And I heard a loud voice from the throne that said, Look, the encampment of God among men, and he will put up his tent among them, and they shall be his peoples and God himself shall be with them, their God, and he will wipe away every tear from their eyes, and there will be no death any more, and no grief, and no crying, and no pain any more; the old world has gone. And he who sits on the throne said, Look, I make all things new. And he said, Write, that these words are faithful and true. And he said to me, It has happened. I am the A and the Z, the beginning and the end. I shall give freely to whoever is thirsty for a drink of the spring of the water of life. The winner will inherit this, and I will be his God, and he will be my son. But the cowards and the unfaithful and the filthy and the murderers and whores and the drug-dealing magicians and idolaters and all false people will have a share of the burning lake of fire and sulphur. That is the second death.

And one of the seven angels who have the seven bottles full of the seven last strokes came and said, Here, I will show you the bride, the wife of the Lamb. And he carried me away in the spirit to a great, high mountain, and showed me the holy city of Jerusalem, coming down out of Heaven from God, with the glory of God; her light was like the most precious stone, like the crystalline jasper stone; she had a great, high wall with twelve gates, with twelve angels at the gates, and names inscribed, which are the names of the twelve tribes of the children of Israel: three gates on the east, and three gates on the north and three gates on the south and three gates on the west. And the city wall has twelve foundation stones, and on them the twelve names of the twelve apostles of the Lamb. And the one who spoke to me had a measure, a golden reed, to measure the city and its gates and its wall. And the city is square, its length is the same as its width. And he measured the city with his reed at twelve thousand furlongs; its length and width and height are equal. And he measured its wall at a hundred and forty-four units, by man's measurement, that is by an angel's. And the material of the wall is jasper. And the city is pure gold, like pure glass. The foundation stones of the city wall are decorated with every kind of precious stone. Its first is jasper, the second is sapphire, the third chalcedony, the fourth emerald, the fifth sardonyx, the sixth sardis, the seventh chrysolite, the eighth beryl, the ninth topaz, the tenth chrysoprase, the eleventh hyacinth, the twelfth amethyst. And the twelve gates are twelve pearls, that is, each of the gates was made of a single pearl. And the city square was pure gold, glittering like glass. And I saw no temple in it, because the Lord God the Almighty and the Lamb are its temple. And the city has no need of the sun or the moon to shine on her, because the glory of God is her light and the Lamb is her lamp. And the nations shall walk in her light, and the kings of the earth bring their glory to her. And her gates shall not be closed by day (because there will be no night there), and they will bring her the glory and honour of the nations, and nothing common shall enter her and no one who makes filth or falsity, but only those who are written in the Lamb's book of life.

# CHAPTER
## 22

AND HE SHOWED me a river of the water of life as bright as crystal, that ran out from the throne of God and of the Lamb, in the middle of the city square. And on both sides of the river grew the tree of life, which carried twelve fruits, and yielded fruit every month, and its leaves were for the healing of the nations. And there will be no curse any more, and the throne of God and of the Lamb shall be in it. And his slaves shall serve him, and see his face, and his name shall be on their foreheads. And there will be no nights any more, and they have no need of lamplight or of sunlight, because the Lord God will shine on them. And they will reign as kings for ages of ages.

And he said to me, These words are faithful and truthful, and the Lord God of the spirits of the prophets has sent his angel to show his slaves what must happen quickly. And look, I am coming quickly. Blessed is he who keeps the words of the prophecy of this book.

And I am John, who saw and heard all this. And when I heard it and saw it, I fell down to worship at the feet of the angel who showed me these things. And he said to me, Watch out, do not do that. I am your fellow slave, and one of your brothers the prophets and those who keep the words of this book; worship God.

And he said to me, Do not seal up the words of the prophecy in this book, because the time is close. Let the wicked man go on with his wickedness, and the just man go on with his justice, and the holy man go on with his holiness. Look, I am coming quickly, and my wages are coming with me, to pay everyone according as their actions are. I am A and Z, the first and the last, the beginning and the end. Blessed are those who have washed their clothes, so that they will have power over the tree of life, and at the gates to enter the city. Outside will be dogs and drug-dealers and whores and murderers and idolaters, and everyone who loves falsity and creates it.

I am Jesus. I have sent my angel to witness to you about these matters for all the churches. I am the stem and race of David, the bright star, the morning star.

And the Spirit and the Bride say, Come. And let whoever hears say, Come. And let whoever is thirsty come, let whoever wants it receive the water of life and receive it free.

I am a witness to everyone who hears the words of the prophecy of this book. If anyone adds to it, God will add to him the strokes written in this book, and if anyone takes away any words from the book of this prophecy, God will take away his share of the tree of life, and of the holy city, which are written in this book.

The witness to this says, Yes, I am coming quickly. Amen, come Lord Jesus.

The grace of the Lord Jesus be with the saints. Amen.